W9-BON-243

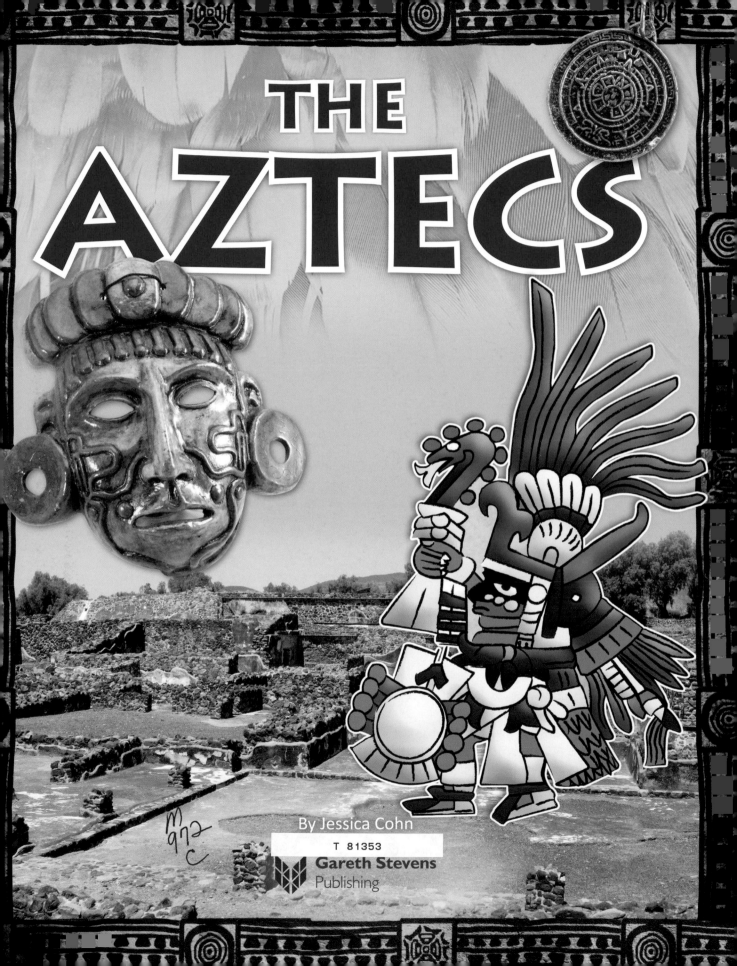

THE AZTECS

By Jessica Cohn

Gareth Stevens
Publishing

Please visit our website, www.garethstevens.com. For a free color catalog of all our high-quality books, call toll free 1-800-542-2595 or fax 1-877-542-2596.

Library of Congress Cataloging-in-Publication Data

Cohn, Jessica.

The Aztecs / Jessica Cohn.

p. cm.　　(Crafts from the past)

Includes index.

ISBN 978-1-4339-7714-5 (pbk.)

ISBN 978-1-4339-7715-2 (6-pack)

ISBN 978-1-4339-7713-8 (library binding)

1. Aztecs History Juvenile literature. 2. Aztecs Social life and customs Juvenile literature. I. Title.

F1219.73.C62 2013

972'.018dc23

2011052732

First Edition

Published in 2013 by

Gareth Stevens Publishing

111 East 14th Street, Suite 349

New York, NY 10003

© 2013 Gareth Stevens Publishing

Produced by Netscribes Inc.

Art Director Dibakar Acharjee

Editorial Content The Wordbench

Copy Editor Sarah Chassé

Picture Researcher Sandeep Kumar G

Designer Ravinder Kumar

Illustrators Ashish Tanwar, Indranil Ganguly, Prithwiraj Samat and Rohit Sharma

Photo credits:

t = top, a = above, b = below, l = left, r = right, c = center

Front Cover: Netscribes Inc., Shutterstock Images LLC Title Page: Shutterstock Images LLC

Contents Page: Netscribes Inc. Inside: Netscribes Inc.: 4, 5b, 6, 7tl, 7tr, 7bl, 7br, 9t, 9b, 11t, 11cl, 11cr, 11bl, 11br, 15t, 15cl, 15cr, 15b, 17t, 19t, 19cl, 19cr, 19bl, 19br, 20, 23t, 23cl, 23cr, 23bl, 23br, 27tl, 27tr, 27bl, 27br, 28, 31t, 31cl, 31cr, 31bl, 31br, 35tl, 35tr, 35bl, 35br, 38, 39tl, 39tr, 39bl, 39br, 43t, 43cl, 43cl, 43cr, 43bl, 43br Shutterstock Images LLC: 5t, 8, 10, 13t, 13b, 14, 16t, 16b, 17c, 17b, 18t, 18b, 21, 22, 24, 25t, 25b, 26t, 26b, 29t Vladimir Korostyshevskiy, 29b, 30t, 30b, 32cl, 32cr, 32b, 33 Jose Gil, 34, 36, 37t, 37b, 40, 41t, 41b, 45br, 48b IstockPhoto: 12 NASA, ESA, and A. Aloisi (Space Telescope Science Institute and European Space Agency, Baltimore, Md.): 42b

Printed in the United States of America

CPSIA compliance information: Batch #CS12GS: For further information contact Gareth Stevens, New York, New York at 1-800-542-2595.

Contents

A New Land

Long ago, the Aztecs lived on an island north of what is now Mexico. According to **legend**, their god told them to go where the cactus grows. They left their home and wandered through the Valley of Mexico, looking for land to develop. The best areas were already taken.

Water World

Around A.D. 1200, the Aztecs settled near Lake Texcoco. The area was swampy, so they built canoes for hunting wild game. To grow food, they built gardens that seemed to float in the water.

After this humble start, the Aztecs grew rich and strong. They adapted to their new land and conquered their neighbors.

The Aztec sun calendar tracked days, weeks, and years. The face in the center was the sun god.

The Aztec capital was called Tenochtitlan.

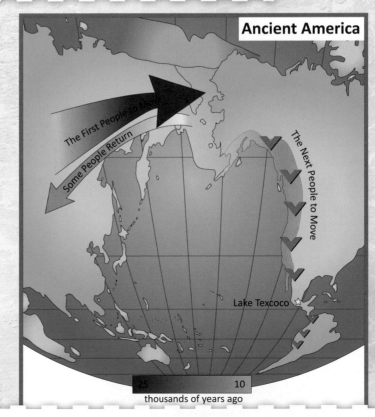

Ancient America

The First People to Move

Some People Return

The Next People to Move

Lake Texcoco

25   10
thousands of years ago

Ancient America was first settled by **nomads** from Asia. They traveled across a bridge of land that used to exist between Asia and North America.

Water Highways

The great city of Tenochtitlan was built on an island in Lake Texcoco. The people traveled mainly by canoe, using canals as roadways. At the height of the Aztecs' power, there were tens of thousands of canoes in and around the great city.

Canoes moved food and other goods to market. They carried warriors to battle. Some canoes were used for garbage and waste.

Close-Up

The Aztecs used dugout canoes, made from solid pieces of wood. A tree was cut, and the bark was removed. The interior was cut out first. Then the outside of the vessel was carved. Average canoes were about 14 feet long. However, others were three times that long.

Canoe for You

You can make a simple canoe from a humble toilet paper tube. Though not cut from a solid piece of wood, your canoe will glide in the same way as a dugout canoe.

Materials Needed
- Toilet paper tube
- Glue and tape
- Book
- Scissors

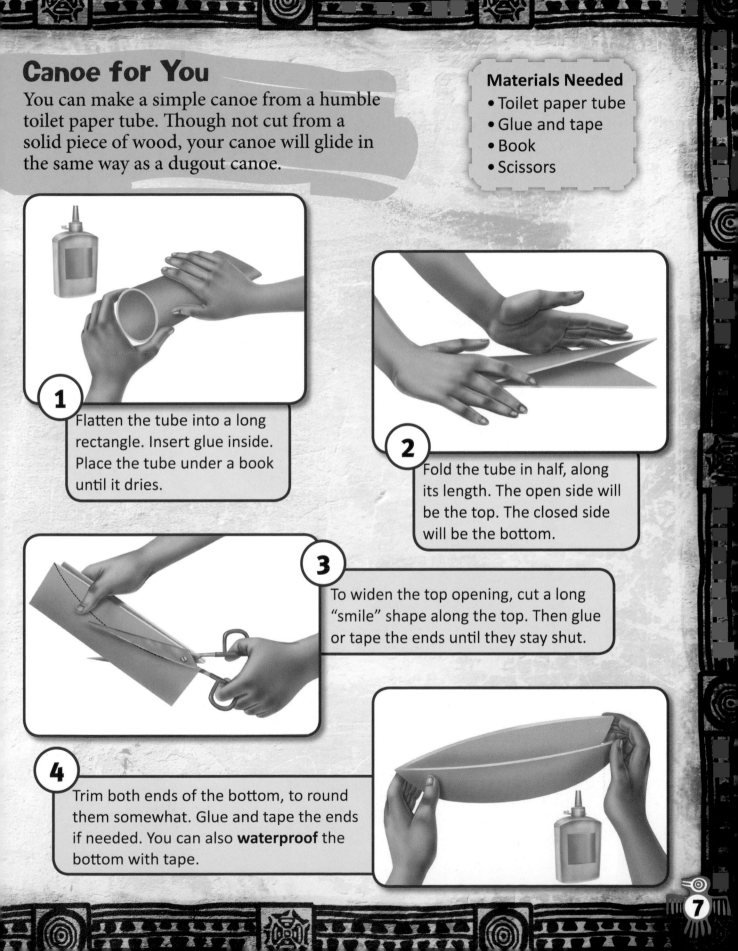

1 Flatten the tube into a long rectangle. Insert glue inside. Place the tube under a book until it dries.

2 Fold the tube in half, along its length. The open side will be the top. The closed side will be the bottom.

3 To widen the top opening, cut a long "smile" shape along the top. Then glue or tape the ends until they stay shut.

4 Trim both ends of the bottom, to round them somewhat. Glue and tape the ends if needed. You can also **waterproof** the bottom with tape.

In the Fields

The Aztecs developed methods that allowed them to grow astounding harvests of corn, cotton, and other crops. They built zoos and flower gardens. Their empire reached as far south as what is now Guatemala. It grew to include three large **city-states** and many others. It stretched from the Gulf of Mexico to the Pacific Ocean.

The Aztecs built a sewer system that recycled waste into **fertilizer** for the gardens.

Wealth of Resources

By **cultivating** cotton, the Aztecs could spin thread and weave fabrics. Their builders cut wood from forests and used mud and stone for bricks.

Workers dug for gold and other important metals, such as copper. They learned to heat and shape the metals into tools, such as ax blades, and works of art.

Each of the city-states had its own Aztec ruler. People brought the rulers gifts.

The main city-states in alliance were Tenochtitlan, Texcoco, and Tlacopan.

Texcoco

Tlacopan

Tenochtitlan

Riches from Nature

The Aztecs ruled over land that was formed, in part, by ancient volcanoes. The people valued the volcanic glass and rocks they found. Dark green rocks and stones, called greenstone, were especially treasured. They included a number of kinds of rocks, such as jade.

Feathers from tropical birds were also highly prized in Aztec society. Then as now, rare items were thought to have value.

Close-Up

The rulers wore headdresses made from the rarest of feathers. The fanciest feathers came from rain forests far from the capital.

Feather in Your Hat

You can make a feather headdress using simple art materials. Look for ready-made feathers at a craft supply store. Or make your own by copying the shape shown.

Materials Needed
- Construction paper
- Scissors
- Glue and tape
- Optional: glitter, markers, beads

1 Cut a strip of paper about 2 inches wide, for a headband.

2 Get someone to fit the strip around your forehead. Tape and glue it to the right size.

3 Cut feather shapes if needed. Slit the sides so they are feathery.

4 Glue and tape the feathers to the band, and decorate as desired.

Common Concerns

Most Aztecs were farmers. The majority of commoners raised food and paid **tribute**, a form of taxes, to the nobles. The nobles had their own work to do. The ruling class was in charge of public works. They supervised the building of canals, temples, and other industrial projects, using slaves for the work.

The Warriors

This was a warring society. Like two great hands, war and **agriculture** held the Aztecs together. The military conquered the people in surrounding lands. They took prisoners and collected tributes. The Aztec military included two units of **elite** soldiers. They were the **Jaguars** and the Eagles.

All males were taught the ways of war, but the great warriors were nobles who were trained for the work.

The Aztecs were raising crops of tomatoes as early as A.D. 700.

Most slaves were captured during fighting, but some slaves were commoners who owed money or committed crimes.

Trading Places

There were several levels of Aztec merchants. Some worked like peddlers, in local markets. Other traders traveled long distances between the city-states, which were known as the **altepetl**. Each altepetl was made up of extended families. These family groups were called the **calpolli**. That means "big house." Each of the groups had a chieftain. The traders were responsible for communication between the chieftains. The traders, called the **pochteca**, were commoners, but they were important in society.

Close-Up

The traders who traveled long distances over the countryside also served as spies. Their dealings made them richer than most people. They lived together, keeping their wealth to themselves. The pochteca even had their own god. He was Yacatecuhtli, god of business and traveling.

Designs of the Time

Pottery was one of many items traded in open-air markets. To make your own Aztec pottery, start by looking at the items in your recycling bin.

Materials Needed
- Recycled can
- Scissors
- Brown paper bag
- Can opener if needed
- Paint or markers
- Glue

1 Look throughout this book at the Aztec art. Pay attention to the designs that you see.

2 Cut an even strip from the bag, big enough to roll around and cover the side of the can.

3 If the can was just punched open on one end, finish removing that end, using the opener.

4 Make Aztec designs on the strip, and then glue it to your new Aztec pencil can.

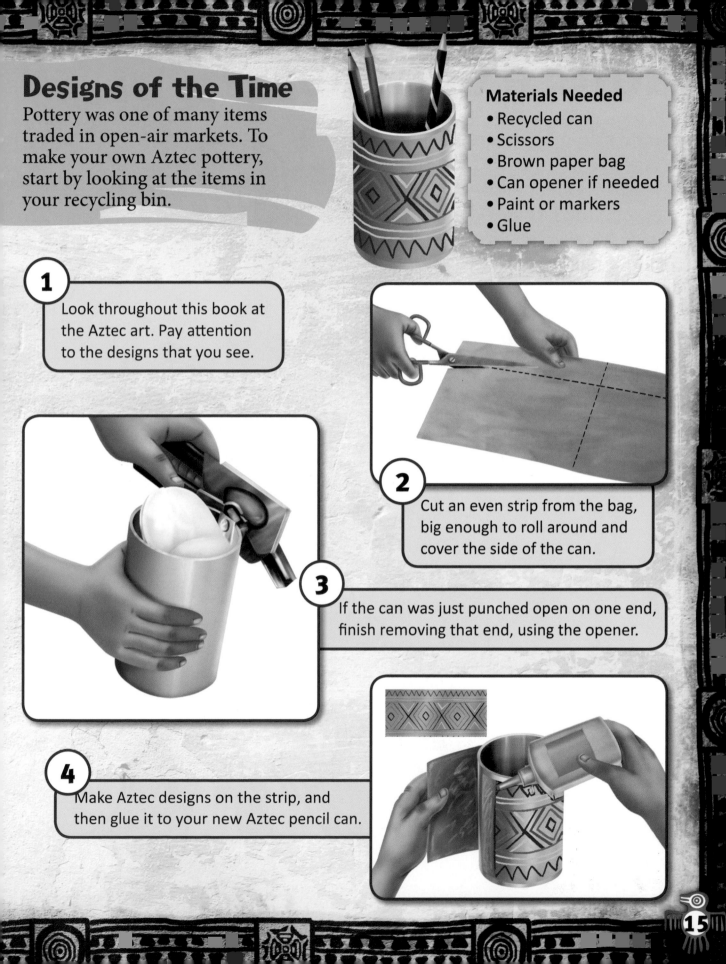

Nature of Belief

According to legend, the god who guided the Aztecs to Lake Texcoco was Huitzilopochtli, the sun god. The fact that the Aztecs were so dependent on farming was reflected in their beliefs. There were gods for the sun, corn, and running water. Their gods often stood for parts of nature.

Huitzilopochtli was also a god of war.

Life on Earth

The people believed that life was possible because the gods gave up their lives at the start of history. To pay back the gods, the people offered precious gifts, called sacrifices.

Of All Creation

Like all people, the Aztecs told myths about the creation of the world. One story was about five suns. The first four suns stood for four ages that ended in destruction. The fifth age, in which the Aztecs lived, was started when a small god named Nanahuatl jumped into a fire and became the sun. Nanahuatl became Huitzilopochtli.

The god of night was Tezcatlipoca, a brother to Quetzalcoatl, god of the sky.

Another god named Tecciztecatl was jealous of the sun god but too afraid to jump into fire. He became the moon.

Cult of the Serpent

When the Aztecs arrived in the Valley of Mexico, they met and mixed with people who were already there. The people shared stories, including tales of a kind god named Quetzalcoatl. He was related to the wind and seen as a feathered serpent. The people sacrificed butterflies and hummingbirds to him.

Representations of Quetzalcoatl are found in the Aztec ruins.

Close-Up

In modern America, people pay taxes to pay for the benefits of being in society. The Aztecs paid in gifts called tributes. One common tribute was the gift of masks. The masks were used for **rituals**. They were used for ceremonies for the many gods.

Tile Smile

A famous mask of Quetzalcoatl is in the British Museum. It is a mosaic of **turquoise** with teeth made of shells. You can make your own with simple materials.

Materials Needed
- Cardboard
- Markers
- Colored paper
- Glue
- Scissors
- Thin, white recycled plastic, such as a milk carton

1 Draw a large outline of a mask on cardboard. Add the eyes, nose, and mouth.

2 Rip bits of colored paper for tiles. Arrange them and glue them in place.

3 Cut teeth from white plastic and glue them in place.

4 Cut out the mask for hanging on a door or bulletin board.

Great Pyramid

In the capital, the Templo Mayor was where many festivals took place. It was a large **pyramid** with temples on top, built for both the gods of water and of war. The base of the pyramid was 330 feet by 260 feet. Like most public buildings, it was made of stone.

The Templo Mayor is gone. This is an artist's idea of what it may have looked like.

The ruins of the Templo Mayor include a wall of skulls.

Temple District

In the great city of Tenochtitlan, the great pyramid was the largest structure. It was found in the temple district. That was the section of the city filled with buildings for gods. The district was constructed to look like a small region of stone mountains. There were about 70 structures.

Inside Homes

The homes of commoners were one-room huts of wood and loam. Their flat roofs were built from reeds, so when it was hot, the people went on their roofs. Most nobles lived in two-story homes made of stone. The better **abodes** were located near pools. A typical floor plan for a noble's home was shaped like a hollow square, with a courtyard in the middle.

Close-Up

Common people had simple furniture, such as low tables and mats made of reeds. Their homes were **dominated** by the useful items needed to cook and raise food. The nobles had items that were prized for their beauty.

The Aztecs' homes have disappeared, but ruins of houses from people who came before the Aztecs can still be seen.

Paper Pottery

The Aztecs made beautiful dishes, and even simple ones were decorated. Here, you can make an Aztec plate, using what you know about Aztec designs.

Materials Needed
- Paper and pencil
- Paper plate
- Light brown or yellow paint
- Black or dark brown paint
- Paintbrush

1 First, design the plate on a piece of paper. Make shapes on the rim and something big in the center. Look in the book for animals, gods, or other ideas.

2 Paint the plate light brown or yellow. Then let it dry.

3 Use a darker color to make the design in the center.

4 Finish by adding a design to the rim.

Food from the Fields

Corn, squash, and beans grew abundantly in human-made islands, called **chinampas**. The Aztec garden plots are often called floating gardens, because they appeared to float in water. However, the plots were connected to the ground. Workers staked out an area on the floor of the lake. Then it was filled in with dirt.

Gathering Dinner

The Aztecs rode canoes between the chinampas, hunting fish and waterfowl. They also grew crops in large plots on the hillsides outside of town. While the men worked in the fields and canals, the women raised turkeys. They grew additional crops in small plots near their homes.

Beans were important in the Aztec diet. They were important enough to be used as tributes sometimes.

The Aztecs raised both dogs and turkeys for meat.

The waterways around the fields were especially handy when the plants needed watering. The irrigation was built right in.

Corn Meals

The main food was corn, which was ground into flour to make tortillas and tamales. The Aztecs also ate beans and squash. They were fond of chilis, tomatoes, limes, and potatoes, and they enjoyed cashews and peanuts. In addition, the Aztecs collected **algae** from the water. It was used to make a cheeselike food and was added to bread.

Close-Up

The Aztecs grew cacao beans and made chocolate from them. The beans were so valuable, the people used them as a form of money. From the cacao beans, the Aztecs made a chocolate drink spiced with chilis and thickened with corn.

Traditional Mexican cooking today relies on many of the same ingredients used by the Aztecs.

Corn Wrap

Corn was central to the Aztecs and often appeared in their art. You can make corn art, too, using beads and a few other simple items.

Materials Needed
- Beads in yellow, orange, beige, red, brown
- Two 6-inch chenille wires, sometimes called pipe cleaners
- Scissors
- Raffia or ribbon

1 Make an X from the wires. Wrap one around the other.

2 Now, form a "rake," with a handle and three prongs.

3 String beads on the prongs. Then bend them together at the bottom to shape them into a "cob."

4 Wrap raffia around the top in a bow. Then, bend the "handle" into a loop to hang your beaded corncob.

Fabric of Life

The rich wore clothing that was woven from cotton. Women wore wrap dresses or long **tunics**. Men had **loincloths** and added tunics or other shirts when the weather was colder. Poor men wore plain loincloths made from plant fibers. Rich men wore cotton decorated with shells, feathers, and fancy stitching.

Seeing Red

Wealthy men had hair to the shoulders, with straight bangs. The warriors wore ponytails. The women favored long hair and braids. The wives of warriors cut their hair short and often dyed it a reddish color. Sometimes they dyed their feet and painted designs on their hands and necks.

In America, descendants of the Aztecs perform in native dress at various festivals.

The Aztecs valued red dye made from a kind of beetle.

The climate was warm, so the clothing fit loosely.

Status Items

There were rules about what people could wear. Only the royals could wear headdresses made with the feather of the quetzal, a kind of bird. The warriors used lip plugs, which were large inserts in the lips. Famous warriors often had plugs in the shape of animals.

Close-Up

The people who were skilled with their hands made jewelry from gold and silver. They made ornaments from feathers, shells, stones, and leather. As with clothing, only important people were allowed to wear fancy things.

Men wore plugs in their lips, noses, and ears.

Art on a Shoestring

Wealthy Aztecs used shells for decoration, but it is not costly to make a shell necklace of your own. The shells are found at craft stores or restaurants that serve seafood.

Materials Needed
- Long, high-top shoelace
- Flat seashell, such as a clamshell
- Glue gun
- Paper and pencil
- Glitter, paint

1 Tie the shoelace shut with a double knot.

2 Glue the knot to the back of the shell.

3 While the glue is drying, create a design for the shell on paper.

4 Decorate the shell, using paint, glitter, or other art supplies.

Aztec Arts

The Aztecs showed a love of beauty and balance in their arts. Artists **transformed** clay into statues of warriors and gods. They made gold into ornaments and other lasting treasures. The artists developed ways to work with materials from the land, such as obsidian. That is a shiny black glass formed from volcanoes.

Aztec designs remain as part of Mexican culture.

Live Performance

The Aztec year was filled with festivals that celebrated the gods. The public events featured live performances. Dancers and **acrobats** acted out stories. Musicians played music, and poets weaved words together, making what sounded like spoken music. The best poets took part in contests. The gatherings followed the change of the seasons.

Modern Day of the Dead festivals keep elements of the Aztec festivals alive.

Beat of the Drum

Rattles, shakers, and drums were the main instruments. Aztec music was filled with the sound of **percussion**. The musicians also played wind instruments made from gourds and shells. They performed on smaller flutes and whistles made of clay. The clay ones were often shaped like animals.

This clay Aztec warrior is actually a flute.

Close-Up

The festivals also featured some kind of sacrifice. Sometimes humans were killed and offered to the gods. Yet other kinds of rituals were far less **gruesome**. For example, when it was time to plant new crops, the people offered flowers.

Note by Note

The basic principle of wind instruments is to control airflow. You can make a very simple flute from a single straw.

Materials Needed
- Plastic straws
- Scissors
- Hole punch

1 Flatten the straw, especially at one end. Then cut a dart shape at that end.

2 Make two or three holes along one side of the straw. See how it sounds.

3 Experiment by cutting other straws that are shorter.

4 Try making a "trombone" by slipping one straw over another.

Play Ball

The Aztecs played a game called **tlachtli** on a field shaped like an H. The goal was to move a rubber ball to the opponents' side, and this was often done using only hips and feet. Each team had to guard a stone ring, because players scored by getting the ball through its center.

At each end of the field, there was a wall.

Serious Sports

Children played games for fun. However, the most important sports were tied, like most things, to religious festivals. Commoners did not play at the ceremonies, but they took part by betting on them. The ballplayers were looked up to in Aztec society.

Tlachtli survived the Aztecs. There are courts that are still standing.

The players wore padding.

Game On!

Aztecs connected their sports and games to religious practices. They were fond of a board game called **patolli**, and players prayed to the god of patolli. The board was shaped like a cross with many sections. The competitors had four or five beans marked with signs that stood for numbers. The beans worked in the way that dice do, to move the pieces along.

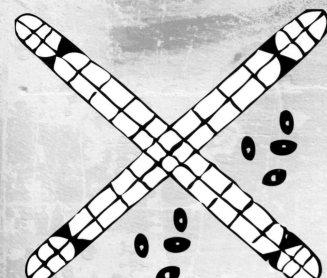

Game boards were made on reed mats that could be rolled up.

Close-Up

Aztec children had contests with bows and arrows. It is clear that they played marbles, too, because old clay marbles have been found. They probably played in much the same way that the game is played now, in that one player knocked the other's playing pieces out of action.

Making Clay *

On the next page, you will find instructions for making your own marbles from self-drying clay, which you can buy from a store. To make your marbles even more authentic, you can use this simple recipe for homemade clay:

i Mix 4 cups all-purpose flour, 1 cup salt, and 1 ½ cups water. It's easy! However, if you do use homemade clay, you will need to dry your marbles in the oven, with the help of an adult.

ii For Step 2, dry the marbles in a 350-degree oven for about 45 minutes. Then color them.

(Note: Ask an adult for help with the oven.)

All My Marbles

Marbles have been found in ancient sites around the world, not just among the Aztecs. Any time in history is a good time to make your own fun with homemade marbles.

Materials Needed
- Self-drying clay*
- Paint and paintbrush
- Chalk

1 For each player, form ten balls of the same size. Make one larger one.

2 Allow the clay to dry. Mark or color each player's marbles with identifying color.

3 Draw a ring on a sidewalk with chalk. Place all marbles in the center.

4 Take turns. Use the large marble as a shooter to knock the opponent's marbles from the circle.

Class in Session

What was life like for young people? At age 15, the male children of nobles went to special schools. They were taught history, religion, and the art of war. Some were sent to schools to learn about religion and government. Others went to schools that **emphasized** military training.

Girl Talk

Around the age of 12 or 13, the female children of nobles spent a year in the temples. They were given religious instruction. A few of the girls became part of religious life after that. They took part in religious ceremonies. However, most returned home.

Quetzalcoatl was also the god of learning and knowledge.

Home Schooling

Before students were sent to school, they were taught by their mothers and fathers. Parents taught their children basic skills, such as weaving and farming. The children were taught right behavior from wrong behavior.

The Aztec temples are no longer standing. The remains of the temples in Tenochtitlan, for example, are surrounded by newer structures.

The male students were taught to be warriors, and the schools had rivalries.

Ancient Studies

The children of people who worked in trades, such as construction, were sent to trade schools. The schools for workers were called the **telpochcalli**. Students learned fundamentals of religion. If they stood out in their studies, they were sent to study with the nobles. The schools that the nobles attended for advanced studies were called the calmecac.

Place Yourself in Tenochtitlan

Which school would you want to go to?

The Aztecs made advances in astronomy.

Close-Up

The subjects taught in the calmecac included statesmanship, or how to run the government. Students learned about astronomy, or what was known about the stars and planets. They studied math, writing, and religion.

Counting the Days

One kind of Aztec calendar had three rings. The outside ring showed the days. The middle tracked the weeks. The inside tracked years. Try making a similar tool to see how their calendar worked.

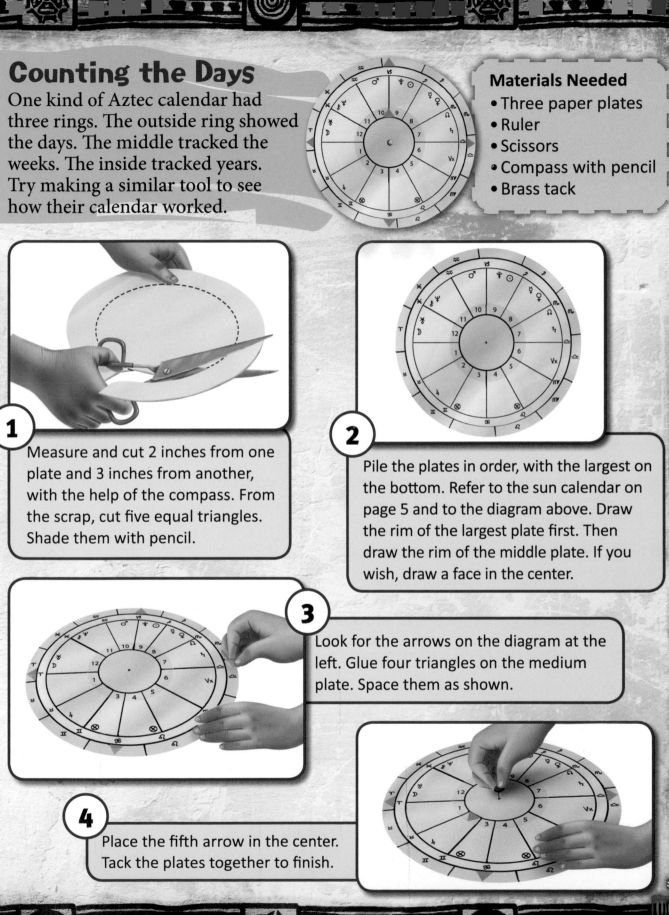

Materials Needed
- Three paper plates
- Ruler
- Scissors
- Compass with pencil
- Brass tack

1 Measure and cut 2 inches from one plate and 3 inches from another, with the help of the compass. From the scrap, cut five equal triangles. Shade them with pencil.

2 Pile the plates in order, with the largest on the bottom. Refer to the sun calendar on page 5 and to the diagram above. Draw the rim of the largest plate first. Then draw the rim of the middle plate. If you wish, draw a face in the center.

3 Look for the arrows on the diagram at the left. Glue four triangles on the medium plate. Space them as shown.

4 Place the fifth arrow in the center. Tack the plates together to finish.

Glossary

abodes—places where people live

acrobats—people who perform skillful changes of body position

agriculture—practice of producing crops

algae—simple organisms that usually live in water

altepetl—city-states of the time; the local political grouping

calpolli—related group that lives together in part of an Aztec city

chinampas—garden plots built like islands in water

city-states—cities and the territories around them, when they are under one government

cultivating—fostering the growth of something

dominated—commanded by having a better position or having more of something

elite—group that exercises power over others; also, powerful or having influence

emphasized—stressed

fertilizer—material that helps something else grow

gruesome—inspiring horror or disgust

jaguars—large cats found in Central and South America; name of elite Aztec warriors

legend—story that has been passed down

loincloths—simple coverings for the area around the hips

nomads—people who move from place to place

patolli—type of board game played by the Aztecs

percussion—striking an instrument to make sound; also, that type of instrument

pochteca—long-distance Aztec traders

pyramid—structure, usually with a square bottom and four triangles for walls that meet at a point at the top; Aztec pyramids had a flat top where temples were built.

rituals—ceremonies; customary ways of doing things

telpochcalli—Aztec schools for trades

tlachtli—type of ancient sport played on a field with a rubber ball

transformed—changed; remade

tribute—gift that is a kind of payment

tunics—simple garments, with no sleeves, that slip on over the head

turquoise—blue-green mineral that can be polished

waterproof—to coat so water does not seep in; to be able to keep water out

For Further Information

Books

Ballplayers and Bonesetters: One Hundred Ancient Aztec and Maya Jobs You Might Have Adored or Abhorred. Laurie Coulter. (Annick Press, 2008)

History News: The Aztec News. Philip Steele. (Candlewick, 2009)

The Aztec Empire. Robert Hull. (Gareth Stevens, 2011)

The Gruesome Truth About the Aztecs. Jillian Powell. (Rosen Publishing, 2011)

Websites

Ancientweb.org: The Civilizations of Ancient Mesoamerica
http://ancientweb.org/explore/country/Mexico

This online reference tool discusses the Aztecs, Toltecs, Mayans, Olmecs, and other ancient people of North America.

PBS: Conquistadors
www.pbs.org/opb/conquistadors/home.htm

The Oregon Public Broadcasting System offers online video and thoughtful reading about the Aztecs and their conquerors.

Indians.org: The Aztecs/Mexicas
http://www.indians.org/welker/aztec.htm

Information about the Aztec calendar, the game of patolli, and much more is found on a site run by the American Indian Heritage Foundation.

The Sport of Life and Death: The Mesoamerican Ballgame
http://www.ballgame.org/

Learn the meaning of "winner takes all" in this online journey into the ancient spectacle of athletes and gods.

Publisher's note to educators and parents: Our editors have carefully reviewed these websites to ensure that they are suitable for students. Many websites change frequently, however, and we cannot guarantee that a site's future contents will continue to meet our high standards of quality and educational value. Be advised that students should be closely supervised whenever they access the Internet.

Index

Things to Think About and Do

Final Word

One of the things that Aztec children learned in school was the "sayings of the old." These were proverbs that carried lessons that parents wanted their children to know.

They were many answers to one main question:

How do we maintain our balance while walking on the slippery earth?

Not surprisingly, one of the proverbs went something like this.

Avoid the extremes. Keep to the middle.

Try It!

Think about staying in balance or rooted in the earth. Try writing your own proverbs.